INDEX OF HAUNTED HOUSES

POEMS

ADAM O. DAVIS

SARABANDE BOOKS

INDEX OF HAUNTED HOUSES

Library of Congress Cataloging-in-Publication Data

Names: Davis, Adam O., author.

Title: Index of haunted houses / poems by Adam O. Davis.

Description: Louisville, KY : Sarabande Books, 2020

Identifiers: LCCN 2019048402 (print) | LCCN 2019048403 (e-book)

ISBN 9781946448668 (paperback) | ISBN 9781946448675 (e-book)

Subjects: LCSH: Ghosts—Poetry. | LCGFT: Poetry.

Classification: LCC PS3604.A955426 I53 2020 (print)

LCC PS3604.A955426 (e-book) | DDC 811/.6—dc23

LC record available at https://lccn.loc.gov/2019048402

LC e-book record available at https://lccn.loc.gov/2019048403

Cover and interior design by Alban Fischer.

Printed in Canada.

This book is printed on acid-free paper.

Sarabande Books is a nonprofit literary organization.

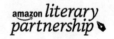

This project is supported in part by an award from the National Endowment
for the Arts. The Kentucky Arts Council, the state arts agency,
supports Sarabande Books with state tax dollars and federal funding
from the National Endowment for the Arts.

FOR MY MOTHER AND FATHER

CONTENTS

INTRODUCTION

The poems of Adam O. Davis's debut collection are epigrammatic, apocalyptic, and downright scary at times. Of course they are. This is a book of ghost stories, and for the most part, ghosts are jealous monsters, intent upon our destruction. They never appear overtly here, yet their presence tiptoes into the book the way we gradually become aware of spirits in haunted houses who tread over creaky floors and slam doors and issue sudden gusts of wind.

Fortunately, Davis recognizes all the standard tropes and approaches his subject in a self-reflective way, coming up with new forms and visionary occupations for the disembodied spirits. They are consistently surprising, convincing, and even delightful. We begin to understand that haunting can be a way of life. And there are metaphoric wonders everywhere: "A spell / of soapy / weather. // A milk-solemn / spinster."

He does all this with compression, play of sound and idea, using classical resources like alliteration, assonance, repetition, and variation. His "tricks" are semantically interesting and daring. Nouns muscle into the job of verbs, as in "This wrist- / watch won't tick, / won't heirloom." He drops words out of sentences, crazily jams phrases together, and somehow all this makes sense in the context of both poem and book. It's a new kind of clarity. Davis's language is spare and tense, and the poems are innovative in the best sense of that word. Reading them, one wonders, Why didn't I think of that?

Woven through the pages are the ghosts of Mary, Jane, and Pat, the disembodied ladies of Bell Telephone's automated message system. They speak of disconnections and wrong numbers, calling up empty houses where signals fail to land or go unanswered. There are photographs too (Davis's own) of abandoned houses and a motel, rough road with a warning sign: "Use at Your Own Risk."

Davis thinks through important matters like place, the persistence of memory, time, and the eschatology of us all. In his obsession with ghosts, he turns to the Middle Ages where "every day was Halloween." He reaches back to the Age of Discovery in the poem "Fever Land, 1499" where "Christopher Columbus woke / and entered the galley / like a fist-fight. *Houses,* // he announced. *Houses, clad in termite / tents, advance across deserts in innumerable / rows of brick and embittered bedlam.*" Though the poems often specify dates, there's an equality to all these hauntings—every instance has its moment, and persists, despite being in the past, present, or future. If there really was a 1980 or 1848 or 1499, Davis implies it is, somewhere. He scans the modern city, suggesting the institutions of our corporate-driven, consumer-oriented world are the real monsters, towering over our "taxi-infested night." The planet Earth becomes "a blue penny   in a black pool." Traffic signs are turned on their heads, "Green for go. Red / to falter. Yellow, I forget."

He writes, "The night is no place for a people whose bodies are purses of smoke." But there is light inside the gloom and doom. Not all ghosts are murderers and clamorers. They can be benign too, lonely and trying to communicate. Perhaps they *are* evidence of an afterlife or, at the very least, memories that persist, that can be shared with others. It's a touching idea.

Index of Haunted Houses is a stunning debut, one that will surprise, convince, and most of all, delight.

—*Sarah Gorham and Jeffrey Skinner, 2019*

INDEX OF HAUNTED HOUSES

Think of this: When they present you with a watch they are gifting you with a tiny flowering hell, a wreath of roses, a dungeon of air. . . . They aren't giving you a watch, you are the gift, they're giving you yourself for the watch's birthday.

—JULIO CORTÁZAR

Years, like any other measure of time, offer mankind the promise of isolate events, of an origin and terminus to history, when in reality there is no isolating time as time has no origin or terminus. 1980 never existed, or, if it did, it has always been 1980.

—MURIEL ÉCHECS

After all, the chief business of the American people is business. They are profoundly concerned with producing, buying, selling, investing, and prospering in the world. I am strongly of the opinion that the great majority of people will always find these the moving impulses of our life.

—CALVIN COOLIDGE

THE BELL SYSTEM

Goodnight—Mary, Jane, Pat.
Sleep tight, you sweet operators

of America, your voices strung
like laundry across this nation

drowsy with a full century's worth
of light. There's nothing you

can't tell me that I haven't already
heard gift-wrapped in your General

American grace, but still I wonder
in what chamber of a horse's ant-

eaten skull I'll recover my youth.
Our human garden grows rich

in these green suburbs and what I feel
is not so much loss as a lessening,

as if the self was nothing more
than a late-model sedan crossing

the city limit in search of a better
resale value. It's funny, this franchise

1

of molecules that fizzes up in each
of us, like motels viral along the interstate:

some full while others flicker and die.
When will the stars rain down

like cheap plaster? When will language
be little more than a dandruff shaken

from our heads? Ladies, you tell me
the number I've been calling has been

disconnected, but where did the person
it belonged to go? Alone on the line

I find only a prairie alive with funneled
wind, a nation heavy with wheat and light,

its chorus of dim voices locked in a kind
of pharmaceutical sleep. I find a system

unchanged, charged with electrical pulses
that send the receiver scurrying in their cradle,

the longhand breath of ghosts rising
through switchboards to ask *Who's there?*

Well, tell me. Who is there? Who goes?
Ladies, please wake up. I want to try again.

THE BODY OF NEW JERSEY, ~~1980~~

The body of New Jersey is sleepy.

      The sky of New Jersey
is imitation crocodile.

     The people of New Jersey hold sunburn
by its delicate hand and say grace in the consequent light
of their television sets.

     In the morning sometimes a sparrow
arrives at a window to ask for a dram of salt.

      Politeness is absurd
but bad manners won't do come teatime.

      Right then the people
of New Jersey listen to the body of New Jersey underneath
the sky of New Jersey.

     No longer can they ignore the gin mills
smoldering like an East European drama.

      No longer can
they rake leaves.

They weep openly in their backyards, beneath
their smokestacks and overpasses, all sweetly candid under
the fast sorrow of the tax collector's case.

                              The air is empty,
as it always is.

             The air that has no voice though we bully it
with flight and forest fires.

                  At the television's supper table
we are still at odds with the sparrow.

                         The sparrow, who sings.

MANIFEST DESTINY

This house will
        outlast
me and all those ghosts
      I know.

      I know
there is always
           a ghost
idling on the edge
       of what
I hold dear.

*

I never know
        when
I should confront
         the ghost
or how to walk
        so that
the ghost leaves
        before
I have to.

*

Please tell me
     how
to smile knowing
          how
terrible the stars
     are for
never changing
       and for
not knowing how.
          Terrible
how terrible
     please
tell me are
     the stars.

METEOROLOGY INDEX

Between absinthe and Corinthians,
between linoleum

        and Lamanites,
ghosts—what else? Ghosts
and more ghosts.

        Ghosts who haunt
the salt shaker and sugar bowl,
who howl like pesos

        as you pass.
Ghosts who speak of skulls
in careful English,

        who smoke
cigarettes indoors, whose heads
are titled by a toxic lack

        of locks.
Ghosts who write love letters
to ghosts, who linger light

        as book-pressed
butterflies upon the lips
of the living,

who taste of lye
and lollipop alike, who stand—
who always stand—

behind you
like a lightning-crippled tree.

NEBRASKAN BRIBES

> Not once

and a river yet: a rapid run

of reckless mouths gnash
their way through the alphabet's

many motorways.

> The crowd—

faces like hot dominoes
in doldrums (their destiny

too dense to parse, too dear
to describe)—is in denial.

*

Give them this day before
they chew even

> the scenery,

before they crush the shunts

that keep the sky in its place
and squash the sarsaparilla

tufts of cloud that congeal
at the eye's very edges.

                        Give
them the blood, the bread,

the ghost, the salty tines
of Satan's seasick fork—

        it's hot:
open a window or something!

I feel the heat of a holy oven
upon my household.

*

To care
is to sometimes kill

as we have sometimes
been told.

        To care
is to carve the image

of our care-
            taker

into this idle tree
and border crossing.

*

Under how many watts
must this age be broiled?

Douse me in better water
for brisker belief.

                Do this
in remembrance of

our impractical head
and heads, our

                illiterate
heart and hearts.

GHOST OF MACONDO

The sea is nowhere

near and still

it separates us.

The sea, sickened

of its place, packed

up its gray suit

and left.

There is no Gulf

of Mexico, just

thousands

of thirsty fish,

flapping in the sun.

SLOW CITY BONES

The body is a cinder-
        block
smashed
    by hydrogen
and moth-light.
        Memory
    a thing
that devours
        things
that will devour
    things.

SPIRIT ARITHMETIC

One nick.
Two nick-

els. Three lic-
orice twists before

bedtime. Four hours
of a leaky faucet. Five times

five times now. Six spoons I swallow.
Seven scratches upon the sun. Eight elms

invisible to the eye. Nine knots in a blonde braid.
Ten attics in this house. In this one we store strangers.

HAUNTED HOUSE, 1780

In August the sun held a coin to the silverberries. They ripened
to cake among the gunshot, among the wounded with their
piecemeal apples and parchment lips. Big houses rose bright as
bezants from the soup bones of that bayou. In the cellars of the
earth gandy dancers danced, singing, *Gulp what the fountain
gives, give this in return.*

GHOST OF MOTEL 6

                If this boy

you inhabit is a hotel,
                        its neon needles

the alphabet lightly. Bibles loam

unopened in the boredom
of bedside tables, patient little loaves

                of leather, black

in their theaters of compressed sleep.

*

In each room
        of each lung,
                        silence swells
                        like a syndicate of ants.

        A ghost unfurls

like a flower from the television. The bathroom
window broken, the wind asking questions.

                               Asking you to come outside,
to see what it has against you.

EXTINCTION DAYS, 1873

Bison skull, seven
standing men

tall. Winter: quavering

fields of damp
wheat, dull breath

of ghosts eases

the embers. Skins
sleep on the backs

of the sleeping.

THE MOSQUITO MONOCRACY

1.

Josephine, I've junked
a jazz band, some squall
grullo by the cobweb's logic.
All skulls and bouillabaisse
but we'll see come Zulu
time if it's of goodwill
or gall the Zoroaster sings.
All this in the hallway where
July stalls, jetlagged,
in the hallway where
the lemonade light lingers.

2.

Every day was Halloween
in the Middle Ages:
the cravats of betrayed
consiglieri crispened under
Carpathian sun. So long,
Main Street. So sorry.
I've rung you jealous
to say slender things
from this fickle well.

I think it best we go
to bed now.

3.

Roll them bones
at benthic measure.
The bankers of sleep
bicker in the break
room. I find telephones
humming in their buoyant
cases everywhere along
the river, all unanswered;
all when answered yield
the voice that calls
you to waking.

4.

From the calcite
mountains of our mouths.

5.

My time in Malaria,
among the mystic
zombies who dragged

themselves like trash
through the tropics
chanting, *No time*
like this time like
this time to waste,
was accurately reported
as an adventure in
rudimentary calisthenics.
They haunt me like
hemoglobin. From behind
bus terminals they ply
us in paper suits, watch
us like iceboxes.

6.

Upon alkaline lakes we
skate on alkaline skates.
In ermine the eel eats
the eggs of each oak tree.
I eye the exit out into
the taxi-infested night.

GHOST STORY, 1971

No water. No wind. The windmills list black against a meteor-red sky. Here the sun kills 60,000 a year. The train whistle no longer blows. A certain part of town.

HANDSHAKE WEATHER

Poltergeists chew
        tar, kick

cans, call
    strangers

      collect.
   They drown

the radioman
     in his radio.

ROSWELL, 1947

1.

A cake of
    soap.

        A Sopwith
    weather balloon.

A logarithm for
        milk.

        Silent and
            solemn spinster.

      Tarantulas watch
        you like a television.

2.

        A spell
of soapy
      weather.

A milk-
     solemn
        spinster.

You taran-
      tula!

3.

A cake
     of Sopwith

ballast. Balloonist
        logarithms are

    silent and
spinster. Watch

      a television, why
         don't you?

GHOST OF GENERAL ELECTRIC

House, I feel altogether
brisk, bundled in nerves

that won't quiet. Our
bodies blink like traffic

lights. Green for go. Red
to falter. Yellow, I forget.

HAUNTED HOUSE, 1978

The fuse box is a medicine-bank, an ark of home remedies.
The buttons crumble like aspirin, taste like tonic water washed
down with lime. There was a time when life clung like crime to
this place. But we had a cure for that.

GHOST OF POLAROID

Winter is a gaunt
             gimlet,
insomniac in sand,
its new gift,
        blue and skeletal,
thrumming,
        That plague
of clockwatchers,
that lazybones of morning
        commutes!
             Even so
everyone applauds
that green sun
shyly
        at the horizon.
For who can ignore
the Jesus bug
             crossing
the pond?
        And who
hides in clouded soil,
             sinking
to lazier bones?
             No one
is sick; nowhere,

no sickness.

No one.

No one feels sick.

STETSON IN RETROGRADE

As a matter of law, the house is haunted.

—*Stambovsky v. Ackley*, 1991

1.

If a house is haunted like a radio
is haunted   If a body is a radio
of blood   If a body of ghosts
hums like blood over a valley of
bone   If blood is a government
of ghosts   If bones grow green
as cash in the foreign national of
our ghosts   If homes bloom
along the interstate of our blood
If from granaries of bone we rise
in the newspapered dawn   If
amongst the chattering of water
we rise like a benediction over the
auspices of convenience   If
ghosts we rise like ghosts   If
we collect we collect like desire in
a desert payphone   If we ring
If we ring like coins in the cup of
night   If we lie like coins in the
palm of Nebraska   If the sun
is an argument with ghosts   If

the sun's argument plays out in
squares upon the floor of this
home   If the day winds down
like a watch   If heaven is a
horology   If desire is the body
we give the past   If at night
termites tick like time in our bones
If in these bones we find the
body's foreclosure

2.

If in foreclosure we find the math
of our homes   If the math of
our homes is the math of fire
If the math of fire is the math of
money   If the math of money
is a map of interstate rain   If
grief is a cup   If grief is a cup
let me drink from it and be drunk
If drunk   If drunk and
wandering   If thirsty and
moneyed   If coined and
fashionable   If drunk and
wandering like a dog through the
supermarkets of the night   If
I want the question of a home
If I want as a windmill wants the
wind   If I want that lesson
If I want the lesson that breaks me
If I want the desert and its wind
If I want to throw myself to it
If I want never to be seen again
If by the light of dentistry my teeth
anoint ledgers lavish with loss
If in these ledgers every tooth is a
house   If debt is a tooth the
dentist will not pull

3.

If awake   If waking   If
awake in the wake of sleep   If
sore-eyed and stubbled   If
poorly fed yet fee'd   If
coffee'd and quiet   If humming
If awake and humming in the halls
of convenience   If aching
under the auspice of birds whose
voices are feathered and vaulted
and keyed   If of our voices we
build a bank will it not speak
If we atone   If we and our
homes atone   If we sink alone
into the chloroform fiduciary of
home   If we pill and drone
If we alone are alone   If we
tether ourselves to the stones
of our homes   If we sink to
lazier bones   If we believe
bankruptcy is a throne   If along
the rails the whistle no longer
blows

4.

If we choose   If we had chosen
If we better   If we   If
we had been   If we had been
better and awake   If we had
accounted   If we had awakened
from the tax of sleep to the muted
bells of bills that rang like fire in
the foundries of past lovers   If
love   If lovers and we sleep
If like fire we bill the forest for
overages   If for a surcharge we
survive the past   If of the past
If of the past we make a ministry
of the past   If we pass like fire
over the waters of ambition   If
upon those waters we find our
faces and weep   If weeping
stops   If stopping stops   If
the ghost-math of money stops
If named   If a name is cast
like a coin over the auspices of
convenience   If I call a name
will that name call back
If I call will I call collect   If I
collect like credit   If I credit a
ghost

5.

If named for a ghost   If in the
name of all ghosts   If the name
is named that calls all ghosts to
waking   If waking ghosts
If ghosts rise like desire from the
granaries of sleep and dress for the
newspapered dawn   If
newspapered and awake   If
hunted by convenience stores
If alone and named   If
nameless and unknown   If
anonymous as light   If mute
as tax   If a dividend of sun sits
like a loan upon the floor of this
home   If silence is a loan   If
the sun is a school   If ghosts
are a lesson drawn in sand   If
the sun looms like a school of
blood over subdivisions of ghosts
If subdivided   If the desert like
a house of belief is a body
dividended with blood

6.

If belief is a ghost   If blood is
weather   If bones are birds in
a body of fog   If debt is a body
clothed with birds   If the body
is a myth in the municipal pool
If birds gather like fists of cash on
federal clotheslines   If ghosts
tremble on foreign buildings like
cups of fog   If cash is the myth
in the myth of collection   If
myth is a lesson in collective loss
If we are learned and lean   If
we are lessened by learning   If
learning is a lean-to to loss   If
a ghost is a home   If a ghost
is a thing bankrupt of bone   If
land is land only if it is lessoned in
homes   If we like land grow
green with the memory of our
blood   If we grow and with
land   If we be   If land is
If we be and with land never let us
be without   If never without
us our ghosts

PACIFIC AMERICANA

History is a ship

that is sent

into the middle

of this world's

mighty indexes

with the mission

of drowning

its bone cargo—

the weight

of its curious words

too much for conscience

to bear.

Forgive us, history.

We orphan

everything

we touch.

HAUNTED CITY, 1967

Let ghosts move silent as rooks through cities stumbling to life.
Let them bless the buses that creep like penitent mastodons
past the marketplace, bless the windows dark as bituminous
fists. And then bless the sky.

GHOST UNION

On the street corner, a sycamore
moonlights as a martyred saint.

There are days when everything

seems to mean something. There
are nights when the moon is held up

like a convenience store. I watch

the neighborhood. The neighborhood
watches itself. Police don't take kindly

to the paranormal. Even poltergeists

have unions nowadays. I miss you
for the memory of having not

known you for so long, for the way

if you didn't have to leave, dawn
would never enter this room at all.

FEVER LAND, 1499

Christopher Columbus woke
and entered the galley like a fistfight. *Houses,*

he announced. *Houses, clad in termite*

tents, advance across deserts in innumerable
rows of brick and embittered bedlam.

Soon after mutiny revoked

his freedom, his dream died feverishly
in the pockets of Genoese contractors,

whose chivalry left them coatless

after every rainstorm, and the wilds
of America remained a theme

park dedicated to ghost stories.

SPIRIT OF BLACK TUESDAY

The sun spies on
me through the key-

hole. Nettle-boned
and bereft, I eat

money like bread.
The light socket

has two faces
that represent one

emotion. I incur
wrath like an Incan

mask. Mister, give me
your blurry coat of

caffeine. Promise
a moat of molasses

to drink. Shine these
shoes to knives.

Sell me back
my piggybank.

HAUNTED HOUSE, ~~1980~~

Don't you know the body is a fire that sings at night? Our
organs stars that winter in western states? Look at us. Look
at us solemn astronauts, us ants smashed under the sun's
question, us symphonies of coin and skull. Everything is new,
isn't it? Yes, everything is new. Everything is new until it's told.

GHOSTS OF THE BELL SYSTEM

Ringing. Ringing.
Mary, Jane, Pat—

rooms everywhere are
ringing. Rattan

furniture is rotting
along with my

breakfast. Ladies,
my morning bowl

of cereal and glass
of orange juice

ringing. Children
at play are ringing

and the cars that
confront them are

ringing, are slowing
to observe their

ringing, are thinking
of the reclining

chairs that await
them in the junk-

yard, in the locus
of all rot where

everything is rotten,
everything rotting.

Ladies, everything is
ringing as you

always said it would.
But I didn't

know then. I didn't
listen. I knew

neither of rot nor
ringing, and now

your words aren't
ringing—they sustain

pitch. They arc like
swans in my cochlea's

cul-de-sac. They nest
there and I ask you—

ladies, please—for three
more minutes' sleep.

HAUNTED HOUSE, 1692

The night is no place for a people whose bodies are purses of smoke, whose voices ring like cash registers, whose teeth are coins tattooed with the mottos of terrible places. But still you wander: asking after people, asking after smoke.

INTERSTATE DUSK

     Spirits said,
Go west, so we went
of night,
     its cloth
weighted with stars

and desert cities
dressed in fire,
     a fire
further from alarm,
until finally we

followed ourselves
home,
     our footprints
fibs in the sand
that swallowed them.

GHOST STORY, 1848

You are a spy in the rain that falls in your head. You have
become a different person and will never know why. Will you
never know? Will you never know why the weather is a
borrowed room in which you record the commands you will
not follow? When it grows cold you chatter like a telegraph.

GHOST OF NASA

We are aware
of the moon.

We have been
there. On television

I saw a cemetery
of palm trees,

their stumps
silvered in plots

of pinkish dirt.
And the stars—

those terrible
stars—said

nothing. This
sky is not

spite nor ill
spirit nor Cain.

This sky is
forecast and we

are the tower
to oversee it.

BORDER SONG

Night: incumbent.
The sky looks

like a taxidermy of
a sky I once knew.

The horizon is
a red memory

of light. Come,
newly polished

world, and break
these hands.

EASTERN STANDARD TIME, 1890

Winter's cognitive attic leaves

trees like wishbones. They wince
when the wind winds up along

these lonely stretches of calico

wilderness. Edison is our only
confirmation saint. Westinghouse

watches Lake Erie burn. A bell rings

out for baptisms. Another is rung
for the baptized. A third announces

a moment of silence for all those

who chose such a time to profess
their flameproof faith. If you listen

closely you can hear their ashes

ask amnesty for the wind.
Remembrance is the only act

of significance. We fall asleep

by the radio to dream of the air
raids like our fathers before us.

INDEX OF HAUNTED HOUSES

The weather is
in handshakes in here.

Bribes pass

from cloud to
cloud: a black

coin or two,

a Nebraskan letter
to meteorology.

Doors open
like brackish brackets.

Dusk is an interstate
coin locker.

I see a slow-burning spleen

of light, a rose-
bush of bones, calm hands.

Don't we all see
the lights of a city

from farther than we'd like?

A HOUSE UNFIT EVEN
FOR GHOSTS

An ant farm

in ruin

    is an abacus

of rain.

*

Ant farm, your colony

    has withered

    to a filmy

      photocopy of

        its former

    self.

*

A time when

    the stars were

known as

    cholera, the sky

      struck through

    with ruby

      sharkfins,

infectious

and radiant,

at once.

*

Time is

the colony that

farms our ruin.

Time is

the farm

we have yet

to colonize.

So say the

sharks,

ants,

abacuses,

stars.

NATIONAL ANTHEM

1.

    Locusts
eat Ohio alive.

June is the first
month in bank
robbery season.

    Silky
tornado
nestles in
the trash.

Angles of
neckties act
as compasses
for flight.

2.

You will
disappear.

3.

You will feel
the need
to disappear.

4.

In an abandoned lot,
a slow conglomerate
of green tongues
devour a dead bird.

5.

Fill in the blank:
"This new-century
sky is _____."

    a) Noctilucent.
    b) Nacreous.
    c) Lenticular.
    d) Unidentifiable
        as fluoride.
    e) All of the above.

6.

The sky is
          a cinder-
block smashed by
hydrogen
          and moth-
      light.

7.

Wreckage
is a kind
of question.

It asks you
to reconsider
your inventory.

8.

Broken jackknife?
Decoder ring?

Come back.

Milk-white set
of marbles?

Come back.

Boiled shark
jaws? Sloop-load

of clams? Antique
copper broach?

Please, come back.

This wrist-
watch won't tick,

won't heirloom,
but disappoint.

9.

In its abandoned lot,
the dead bird is gone.

Green tongues twist
slowly—

                memory
a thing

            that devours
                things

that will devour
      things.

10.

Spare licks
of lightning
pepper the pan-
handle.

Trees teethe
in a locust
zone.

11.

Come back.

12.

Construction
workers wear
federal orange

vests, smoke
cigarettes in
the noon haze

as they undo
the street's
ceiling. Cars

run on boiled
bones. Smog
rolls in like

a prehistoric ghost
to slumber. At
night our cities

are swallowed
in swamps
of orange light.

Ghosts, federal
as bone, boil
around us.

13.

According to
local sources,
a well-kept lawn
is the simplest
indicator of
economic stability.

Also,
burglars operate
under the night's
braille blanket.

Conversation is
a politic of trivia.

A newspaper is
a politic of a tree.

14.

In the beginning
atoms collided
like German
consonants.

Everything
else stewed in
the oil fields of
Los Angeles.

15.

And ghosts,
federal as bone,
boil still around us.

16.

Already heat has broke
loose of its zoo.

        Children
chew tar, kick cans, call
strangers collect.

        They drown
the radioman in his radio.

17.

Come back. Come back,
children. Come back

and see the Midwest's
checkerboard from

30,000 feet, the smoke
of industry leering like

syrup over the river,
alming the sky of life.

GHOST STORY, 2020

The Earth   a blue penny   in a black pool.

GHOST OF A GHOST STORY

Cast from this neighborhood of ghosts we grow thorough as factory weeds, our scrimshaw shadows strong as iron upon the heirloom siding of rain. Can you hear us? Can you hear us testing the locks, the windows, tonguing our way into the cellars and attics of clouds? Listen. The world is a radio for light.

NOTES

The epigraph by Julio Cortázar is taken from "Preamble to the Instructions on How to Wind a Watch," published in his book, *Cronopios and Famas* (Pantheon Books, 1969). The epigraph by Muriel Échecs is taken from her lecture, "Beckett's Clock: The Anxiety of Math in the Search for History," given at Heidelberg University in what was then West Germany on April 19, 1981. The epigraph by Calvin Coolidge is taken from his speech entitled "The Press under a Free Government," given before the American Society of Newspaper Editors in Washington, DC, on January 17, 1925.

All photographs by author. Page 3: *M—TE—*, Texhoma, Oklahoma. Page 19: *Missing a Board*, Cairo, Illinois. Page 35: *Primitive Road Caution*, Tacna, Arizona. Page 45: *Full Service*, Tacna, Arizona. Page 59: *Railyard in Rain*, Springfield, Missouri. Page 81: *Neighborhood by Night*, Pittsburgh, Pennsylvania.

In "The Bell System" and "Ghosts of the Bell System," Mary, Jane, and Pat are Mary Moore, Jane Barbe, and Pat Fleet, otherwise known as the voices behind the Bell Telephone System's automated messages.

Many of the images in "Meteorology Index" were created in response to the symbols and abbreviations for hazardous materials according to the UK Chemicals (Hazard Information and Packaging for Supply) Regulations 2009.

The title "Ghost of Macondo" refers to the Macondo Prospect, the British Petroleum–owned site of the 2010 Deepwater Horizon oil spill, which, as of this writing, is still considered to be the largest oil spill in history. The oil field itself was named after the fictional town featured in Gabriel García Márquez's *One Hundred Years of Solitude* (Harper & Row, 1970), a town that thrived first in anonymity and then celebrity until a banana plantation was established, leading to Macondo's ruin and eventual abandonment.

"Extinction Days, 1873" refers to the nineteenth-century practice of producing fertilizer from the bones of bison. Current estimates place the number of bison in the United States at 500,000 (the majority of which live on ranches or farms) as compared to an estimated 60 million before 1800.

"Ghost of Polaroid" takes its inspiration from Wallace Stevens's "Banal Sojourn," published in his collection, *Harmonium* (Alfred A. Knopf, 1923).

The sycamore tree in "Ghost Union" owes a debt to Utah's Mary Tree, which, according to Peggy Fletcher Stack's "Remembering SLC's 'Mary Tree,'" was "likely the first and certainly the most well-publicized [Virgin] Mary sighting in Utah" (*Salt Lake Tribune*, December 3, 2010). The image of Mary appeared "on a flat knothole when a large branch was cut off by city workers," and a set of stairs was constructed so that worshippers could "touch the image, which was said to 'weep,' or emit liquid." The tree was twice vandalized: once in 2002, when "a vandal chiseled out a gaping hole where believers said the virgin once appeared," and again in 2009, when "another attacker tried to light the stairs on fire." A Plexiglas-encased photograph of the apparition now rests in place of the defaced image. Stack concludes her article noting that "the Catholic Diocese of Salt Lake City never investigated supernatural claims related to the tree, nor has it had any plans to do so."

"Ghost Story, 1848" was suggested by the story of Phineas Gage, an employee of the Rutland & Burlington Railroad Company. On September 13, 1848, in Cavendish, Vermont, a 13.25-pound iron tamping rod was driven through Gage's head by an accidental explosion. Despite the severity of his injury—and the damage it caused to his frontal lobe—he soon regained his full health, albeit with substantial changes to his behavior. In an 1868 address to the Massachusetts Medical Society, Gage's doctor, John Martyn Harlow, described his patient—known before his accident as a responsible and hard-working individual—as having become a "fitful" and "irreverent" man, "indulging at times in the grossest profanity." Harlow added that "the equilibrium or balance . . . between his intellectual faculties and animal propensities [had been] destroyed." In the years following his accident, before turning to livery work, Gage famously became a one-man museum exhibit, touring New England with his iron rod.

"Eastern Standard Time, 1890" refers to William Kemmler (the first individual executed by electrocution), George Westinghouse (who fought unsuccessfully to keep his alternating current from being employed by the electric chair that killed Kemmler), and the Cuyahoga River (a tributary of Lake Erie so polluted that it reportedly caught fire thirteen times between 1868 and 1969, with the 1969 fire garnering so much attention it was credited with inspiring the creation of both the Clean Water Act and the Environmental Protection Agency).

"National Anthem" adapts certain phrases from the 1890 Milton Bradley board game Peter Coddle's Trip to New York as displayed in Margaret K. Hofer's *The Games We Played: The Golden Age of Board & Table Games* (Princeton Architectural Press, 2003).

ACKNOWLEDGMENTS

Grateful acknowledgment is made to the editors and staff of the publications in which the following poems first appeared, often in different versions and with different titles:

Anti-: "National Anthem" and "Spirit Arithmetic"

Barrow Street: "Meteorology Index"

Bat City Review: "Ghost Story, 1848"

Boston Review: "The Mosquito Monocracy"

CutBank: "Ghost of General Electric," "Haunted House, 1978," "Index of Haunted Houses"

Grist: A Journal for Writers: "Haunted House, 1692"

The Laurel Review: "Border Song," "Ghost of NASA," "Ghost Story, 2020," "A House Unfit Even for Ghosts," "Interstate Dusk," "Roswell, 1947"

Oxford Poetry: "Spirit of Black Tuesday"

POOL: "The Body of New Jersey, ~~1980~~," "Eastern Standard Time, 1890," "Extinction Days, 1873," "Fever Land, 1499"

Sixth Finch: "Ghost of Motel 6" and "Ghosts of the Bell System"

SLICE: "Nebraskan Bribes" and "Pacific Americana"

The Southern Review: "Ghost Union" and "Haunted City, 1967"

Western Humanities Review: "Ghost of Polaroid"

"The Bell System" and "Manifest Destiny" were selected by Eduardo C. Corral for the Poetry Society of America's 2016 George Bogin Memorial Award. My thanks to both that esteemed poet and that invaluable institution for that honor.

I would not be a poet without the encouragement and support of teachers, and I'm indebted to the foresight and generosity of Priscilla Becker, Lucie Brock-Broido, Timothy Donnelly, Richard Howard, Patricia Russell, Maurya Simon, and Connie Voisine. If not for Patricia Russell asking me to read my poem aloud in the eleventh grade, or Maurya Simon encouraging me to forget Club Med and apply to graduate programs, or Richard Howard calling me with the news that would spirit me from the Inland Empire to New York City, who knows where I'd be now?

My deepest thanks to Jericho Brown, Victoria Chang, Diana Marie Delgado, Hayley Heaton, Ilya Kaminsky, and Lytton Smith, who made this book what it is through their visions and revisions. My thanks, too, to the Colrain Poetry Manuscript Conference, Hacienda Serena, and Vermont Studio Center, where important work was done.

Thank you to my colleagues at The Bishop's School, particularly those in the English Department, who kept and keep the promise of letters alive in me. Also, to my students, whose curiosity demands my own, thank you.

Love and appreciation to my parents—who always encouraged me to dream—to my brother and sister—who kept me grounded (often in both senses)—to my friends—who know their own degrees—and to Lauren for her support and for giving me the greatest gifts in my life, Niamh and Maeve, whose creativity and delight humble and hearten me daily.

Finally, thank you to Sarabande and all those there who helped put this book into print. In particular, everlasting appreciation to Sarah Gorham, editor extraordinaire, and Jeffrey Skinner for plucking this needle from the proverbial haystack—your belief renews my own. Thank you for your vision of what poetry can be and your commitment to realizing that vision with every book you publish.

ADAM O. DAVIS's poems have appeared in many journals, including *The Believer*, *Boston Review*, *Gulf Coast*, *The Paris Review*, *The Southern Review*, and *ZYZZYVA*. He was the recipient of the 2016 George Bogin Memorial Award from the Poetry Society of America, and has received grants and fellowships from Columbia University, Western Michigan University, and Vermont Studio Center. A graduate of the University of California, Riverside and Columbia University, Davis lives in San Diego, California, where he teaches English literature at The Bishop's School. He was also once hit by lightning. It felt, more or less, like you'd expect.

SARABANDE BOOKS is a nonprofit literary press located in Louisville, KY. Founded in 1994 to champion poetry, short fiction, and essay, we are committed to creating lasting editions that honor exceptional writing. For more information, please visit sarabandebooks.org.